LYNN !!

(SHOUTING YOUR NAME)

Thanks for reading...

BALANCE**ACT**

Also by Ken Cormier

Balance Act - Chapbook (1994)
God Damn Doghouse - Cassette/CD (1995)
Gravitron, Wash the World Down - CD (1998)

BALANCE**ACT**

KEN**CORMIER**

INSOMNIAC PRESS

Some of the stories in this collection appeared (in slightly different versions) in the following journals: *Exquisite Corpse, Generator, Gone, Sulfur*, and *Synergy*.

A live recording of "Christmas with Grandma" appeared on the College Music Journal's CD compilation, *Certain Damage*, Volume 111.

Edited by Jill Battson.
Copy edited by Melanie Morassutti.
Designed by Mike O'Connor.

Canadian Cataloguing in Publication Data

Cormier, Ken, 1968-
    Balance act

Poems.
ISBN 1-895837-67-7

I. Title.

PS8555.O653B34 2000   C811'.6   C00-930474-6
PR9199.3.C6528B342000

The publisher gratefully acknowledges the support of the Canada Council, the Ontario Arts Council and Department of Canadian Heritage through the Book Publishing Industry Development Program.

Printed and bound in Canada

Insomniac Press, 192 Spadina Avenue, Suite 403, Toronto, Ontario, Canada, M5T 2C2
www.insomniacpress.com

The Canada Council | Le Conseil des Arts
FOR THE ARTS | DU CANADA
SINCE 1957 | DEPUIS 1957

ONTARIO ARTS COUNCIL
CONSEIL DES ARTS DE L'ONTARIO

Special thanks to Julie Letendre (my favorite companion and co-star), Jill Battson, my parents Jean and Paul (who never made love in front of me), Elizabeth Bristow, Matthew Mayotte, Bob Tocionis, Suzanna Mroz, Pamela Hayward, Mike Ravita, Patrick Penta, ElectroComp 200, Decky Alexander, Todd Spencer, Lisa Powers, the City of Bristol, Imperial Whiskey, Jon & Kirsten Kleinman, Brian Sinclair, John Burke, Lisa Samra, Herman Melville, Crispin Glover, Gladys Gabump, and to the memory of Mike Bonito and Geoff Streadwick.

This book is dedicated to
Bobby Cormier & Fred D'Aprile,
for compelling me to listen and learn.

PART**ONE**

Songs & Stories

CHRISTMAS WITH GRANDMA

The last time we had Christmas with Grandma she just about puked, four Manhattans, three gin and tonics, a whole six-pack of Schlitz, cheese, crackers, pickles, meatballs, chicken livers wrapped in bacon, pepperoni, Oreo cookies, tuna melts, green beans, Hawaiian pizza with ham and pineapple, and Uncle Steve shouting at the blank TV screen the whole time, NOW WE GOT IT! THIS TIME IT'S OURS! THEY MAY HAVE WON A COUPLE BATTLES, BUT WE GOT THE WHOLE FUCKIN WAR! and Grandma just leaning on the armrest of our big brown couch, drooling, lifting a drink to her mouth, dragging off a Chesterfield, nodding her head back and forth, "No no no... no no no... he's stupid, this one, you're stupid, you got no brain, the TV's not even turned on, you're shell shocked, you're crazy, you're no son of mine until you get your shit together you hear me?" and Uncle Steve ripping his eyes away from the screen, grabbing a liver bacon hors d'oeuvre by the decorative, green cellophane-wrapped-at-the-end toothpick that sticks through it, tears starting to flow down his cheeks, YOU NEVER LOVED ME, MA, YOU NEVER GAVE A DAMN, WHY DON'T YOU GIVE ME A KISS, MA, JUST A LITTLE KISS, and he bites down on the liver bacon hors d'oeuvre, ripping off the end of the decorative, green cellophane-wrapped-at-the-end toothpick and he makes a funny face, sticking out his lips and he makes some funny noises like, oooooouuuummmmm mommy mommy ooooouuum mommy, and he spits the whole thing at Grandma who moves quickly and deflects the liver bacon hors d'oeuvre with the open palm of her right hand, being careful not to spill even one drop of her gin and tonic, and in one smooth motion she pokes Uncle Steve's left eye, sending him screaming into the kitchen; but what about the liver bacon hors d'oeuvre with the half a toothpick sticking out of it being wolfed down fast and hard by our little Chihuahua, Ahab, who began choking and coughing and making the most horrific noises I've ever heard, sort of a WEEEEEAAAOOUL, WEEEEAAAOOUL, and me getting on all fours, rubbing poor Ahab's throat, trying to sympathize, trying to howl along with him, patting him on the back until I hear Mom shrieking THE TURKEY'S DONE, SOUP'S ON, DINNER'S READY, COME AND GET IT, and running to my place at the table, sitting, waiting for the squash, potatoes, string bean casserole, cranberry sauce, tuna surprise, corned-beef broccoli treats, Doritoes, and oh the turkey, what a huge, malformed thing that Mom brings in and sets on the table, and Auntie Rita starts poking it with her fork from the other side of the table just to scare little cousin Suzie who's five years old and has nightmares about food coming alive and killing her, and Auntie Rita laughs and pokes the thing so it looks like it's shaking and trembling and inching its way toward little Suzie, and Suzie gets this wide-eyed look and grabs the edge of the tablecloth and screams in a high-pitched frequency and shakes her head back and forth, back and forth, faster and faster until her face is a blur and her little pigtails slap her cheeks until they're red and she pulls the tablecloth and her plate and milk glass and my plate and milk glass get jerked into the air and come crashing down on the floor, and Grandma says, "Stop that, Rita, Stop that this instant, I'll have none of this nonsense at the Thanksgiving table," and Uncle Steve, still dabbing at his swollen left eye says, IT'S CHRISTMAS, MA, NOT THANKSGIVING, IT'S CHRISTMAS!

MONSTER MELVILLE

Slapping and giggling with moody and shade tree mental
picture asylum under shade tree Bartleby starve with last bit
of human friendship resentment all down and folding in,
    lasting and hanging in.
This tree from which bark and pages circumemulate
This treason from which reason beholds mighty word and
    slash cut
This same daddy with his jag-bitten nails and ink stains
Rage cut everlasting on the carpet, gathered under
    the leg of his wooden chair.
This woman folded and creased straight

       like the daughter of Wallace Stevens
          who smoked slender cigarettes
   and whose meat-chunk mouth smiled and then frowned,
             whiskey and memories.

WALKING HOME

All I ever heard was the rocks breaking on these metal rails. I used to walk here every day. I would run out the back door and behind the garage. I would stop there to light a cigarette and then I'd slide down the steep path to the railroad tracks. The tracks go on and on, straight ahead — I'm sure you've heard all that. Rocks breaking, me balancing, and every once in a while a train would tear by. My mother told me to stand clear of the trains, because if you were too close you'd get sucked under.

Cigarettes and railroad tracks make a perfect match. Wine and whiskey fit into the picture. Not too far from here an old man named nothing laid himself down to look at the stars, his bottle was empty, and he got sliced in two by a commuter train. There was a story in the paper, no pictures. I went to the spot where it happened, but I didn't see anything. I even got on all fours with my nose to the rails, but there wasn't a trace. To me, that was the saddest part — how quickly something like that could be cleaned up.

I've never jumped a freight train, never wanted to. Anyone can find a comfortable boxcar and sit, eating sardines and singing sad old tunes. That's too fast, too loud. It all begins and then it's over. I'd rather hop from tie to tie, picking up pebbles and throwing them down. I'd rather choose one beam and balance, taking careful steps and focusing all my attention on these black shoes. I'd like to hover somewhere between the engineer, speeding his passengers on their merry way, and the old man, lying down to get his last look at the stars.

Weather doesn't matter much. I'll walk through rain and sleet and heat and fog. All I need is this coat, these black shoes, T-shirt, green pants, and a hat. The hat always changes, don't ask me why. I can never hold onto a hat. They either blow off my head or I trade them away. Sometimes my hat gets stolen, and other times I just wake up and it's gone. But it never takes me long to find a new one — tucked under this rock or hanging off that tree limb. Hats follow me. They give themselves to me. They stick around for a few days, or even a couple of weeks. Then they move on. Hats always move on.

I've had this particular visor for five days now. It's made out of orange plastic, handy for keeping the sun out of my eyes, and the gauzy headband soaks up all the sweat from my forehead. I found it in the parking lot of a certain donut shop. It made me very happy since I had just lost my previous hat — an old derby with a couple holes and threads hanging all around the brim — and I was thinking that a hat might help me through any trans-actions I was likely to make that day. You see, when you wear a hat it calms people's nerves. It lets them off the hook. People would much rather talk to a hat than to another person.

I grabbed the visor up and placed it on my head with-out even brushing it off. I walked into the donut shop and placed my order.

"I'll have a large coffee with cream and no sugar, two glazed donuts and a blueberry muffin."

"No muffins."

She was a beautiful one, with her hair up in a bandan-na, her lips raw and meaty as if they had been mauled in some recent accident, and she must have weighed four hundred pounds.

"That's fine. Just the coffee and donuts."

She took my money. I adjusted the new visor and looked at her through the plastic, all orange and fat. She handed me the coffee and donuts in a bag.

"Good morning."

I felt glad that I had been wearing the visor. There's no telling what might have happened if I was forced to deal with a woman like that face to face. As far as she was concerned, she just sold two donuts and a large coffee to an orange visor with a gauzy headband.

Turning to leave, I sensed that a poem was imminent. You should know that I write poems — at least three per day, and sometimes as many as ten or twelve. I write them and publish them all on these tracks.

I try to keep a small notebook and a pen or pencil in my coat pocket, but these things are almost as difficult to hold onto as hats. I love to use chalk whenever I can get it. Rocks and wood planks and train rails are good alternative writing surfaces. I've never been particularly attracted to spraypaint, but I will use it as a last resort.

I happened to be in possession of a pencil as I ran from the donut shop back to the tracks. I could barely contain myself, shoving the donuts down my throat along with the scalding coffee. I used the wrinkled, white bag:

"Donut Lady" (September 9)
Meat-hook face
four hundred pounds.
I could have loved you in some laundromat.
In some other life,
some other hat,
I could have held you, braced
and kissed you.

I took one more sip of coffee and placed the half-empty cup inside the bag. The bag stood up nicely on one of the railroad ties. I left the poem facing in the direction from which I'd come. That's how I do it. It's very simple, really, to write and publish, just as long as you know where you've been and where you're going.

you are a normal animal

You dream in the shower, steam and hot stream sur-
rounding you. Your noise is the noise of the shower fol-
lowing you. Your breathing is a delicate infant you han-
dle, careful not to drop, staining your fingertips, you
touch,

   your breathing takes on the expression you have
described as smiling, you stop your play, your pupils
dilate, face flattens, your hair stands on end, you leap
backward, strike the air before you, you see brightly col-
ored whorls, turbulent rushing, you look at your right
hand and defecate,

                you are a normal animal.

MARK TIME

Clams, clams
On my little brown carpet
Why can't I picture it?

There's a gambling man inside me
I've got to let him out
His hair looks so nice.

And when it's time to grow feelers
My mystified persona
Will trample you like dirt.

Give me a dirge, boys
The captain drank a bottle
And it threw him overboard.

Four times it took me
Begging her for one kiss
To figure something out.

The beauty of a language
Crippled, scarred, and terrified
Impaled on a chain link fence.

I felt a cold lead weight
The day I lost my clipboard
My glasses crushed and torn.

And love affairs with objects
Simply finding used space
Had to end and stop there.

Tear down, buy now stapler
Pinning up a legend
Magic tape and sparklers.

A tranquil little banker
Tying back his nose holes
Making matters worse.

If flying for no reason
Constitutes a madman
Misery cannot be condemned.

The whole of my reason
Grew and was reduced to nothing
That happens every day.

CRAZY DAY

Granny wakes up with a raspy cough and a nasty ache spiraling from the back of her head where more tangled wisps of cotton hair have uprooted themselves.

Today's the day Granny goes crazy.

She doesn't know it yet but today's the day she breaks down in front of a customer at the little corner store where she works, pulls off her wig and cries until her face is shiny with teardrops and runny mucous from her nose.

"I have no idea!" she'll cry, "I have no idea!" to a mustached man in a brown leather jacket who only wants his milk rung up so he can get back to his television, so he can get back to his empty apartment, no work, nothing to do but watch reruns of *Matlock*, get to *Matlock*, fifteen minutes to *Matlock*, and the lady's gone way too crazy to work the register.

The mustached man won't look directly at Granny, her splotchy bald head gives her the look of the undead, and her voice is a rachety-bubble-throat squeal: "I have no idea! I have no idea!" and there's no manager here, no one to settle her down and finish his transaction, so he'll just nod at her for a minute, leaving his eyes and his money on the counter, two-fifty ought to cover it, and get out of that store before Granny starts to break things.

And she will break things.

But she can't foresee such a day, not as she adjusts her gray-haired wig in the bedroom, first thing every morning, even before she puts on her slippers, hates her old bald head, wants to cry every time she looks in the mirror, get the wig on make yourself human no one likes a bald lady circus freak, white whiskers sprouting from her wrinkled chin, Special "K" every morning — used to tell her children it was good for them.

And when the mustached man leaves her alone, abandoned in her space behind the counter, she will swipe his money, slip it down the front of her blouse and, looking from side to side, knock the register to the floor, laughing, pulling cigarette cartons from beneath the counter and littering Aisle One with Lucky Strikes Viceroys Marlboro Lights Camels Newports Merit Ultra-Lights Chesterfield Kings and Salems, dancing down Aisle Two, punching the air and pulling the Hostess stuff off the racks, displacing the Beef-Jerky display, sliding open all three doors to the cooler, and finally smashing both coffee pots, regular and decaf, against the corner of the hard red coffee counter.

But the morning — this morning — is like any other.

Granny scrubs her teeth, cupped in her numb, puffy hand, numb from bad circulation, and she slips the yellowed dentures into that cold gap of a mouth, the ache in her head, the Special "K", she used to go out on the deck on sunny spring mornings, eat her breakfast in the morning breeze, but these days the sun is too hot and the breeze is too cold, and too much fresh air disorients Granny, makes her late for work.

She gets to work by cab, always by cab, calls the cab at the same time every morning, gets to work at the same time, ten minutes early every morning, switches shifts with Raul — the night boy — and makes sure there's fresh coffee, napkins stocked at the donut rack, newspapers stacked neatly on their shelves; six, seven, eight, nine, ten, twenty, thirty, fifty, seventy, seventy-five, eighty, ninety, ninety-five cents, a dollar, most important to balance the cash, and wait for customers on sore little feet, wishing for a chair or stool behind the counter.

Linda, from the laundromat next door, will find Granny weeping in Aisle Three on the floor in a hurdler's stance, two plastic handles with jagged glass (what's left of the coffee pots), boxes of Bugles Saltines Wheat Thins Cheese-Its and Dinosaur Grahams all around Granny, still punching the air, slicing it to ribbons with her brown and orange plastic-glass weapons.

Linda will dial 911 and wait at the opposite end of Aisle Three, keeping an eye on Granny but never getting too close, never speaking a word, tapping her foot, glancing out the front window, waiting for the emergency team who take too long, those bastards what if there was some real emergency, and Granny knows they're coming, she's quiet now, only surrounding herself with boxes, using her coffee pot handles, building a wall, wishing the breezes were warm and the sun not as strong.

"This morning I sat out on the deck," Granny lies, "and I ate my breakfast. What a magnificent morning," to the medics who nod and say, "Yes!" too loud, "It was beautiful this morning!" too agreeable, "You look like you got a little sun!" not even glancing at her. Liars. The medics are liars. "I don't want to go to the hospital." We know. "I want to sit on my deck at home." But we've got to bring you in. "I want my wig, I don't look human." Just to make sure you're all right. "My shirt is ripped, I need my wig, I can't go outside like this." You look fine, now just relax.

Spend an extra minute in bed, Granny. Don't shudder at your reflection, take it all in. Brush those teeth extra hard in your numb, puffy hand. Eat two bowls of Special "K", and for god's sake, bring your tea out to the deck and bask in the magnificent morning.

Today's the day, Granny.

Today's the day you go crazy.

RECOVERY

He's guiding me like I was his own son
through hallways and over rock formations,
leading me around his freshly plowed fields
and down wooded, leaf-coated paths.
My mind is wrong and his is right.
It's what I know, because to me everything spins off and
    out of the string of balance.
Things scare me too much. My first inclination
is to run and hide my eyes, to shade myself away
from all this that seems able to maneuver
and manage effortlessly,
without even thinking.

My skin, raw and exposed to the cutting,
    the pain-heavy rubbing of airborne miscreants,
    the perfectly licit functions of nature, the mundane
    sounds and sights of a drab day.

At the knock of knuckles on door I melt down
    to my hospital gown.
I grab at his collar and try to stuff my exposed head
    and face into his shirt, his pants.
In the bathroom I am alone, and it is always like
    driving a car solo for the first time,
    reaching desperately over to the passenger seat,
    wishing for fingers to feel flesh,
    breath, cotton, nylon.

        My stream of urine seems a joke, a big stringy
joke protruding from out my most private bit of fleshy
mass. My urine wetting and soaking like some
low-pressure hose, I block the stream with my thumb and

create a vengeful diversion. My pants damp and warm but
quickly cooling, in here I am safe. In here I am funny. But too
long in here begins to frighten him, who is never scared
except for me.

He wipes me off with an alcohol-soaked cloth,
bends me into an arc in the heat of a single floor lamp.
My slick torso steams and reflects yellow light in a fuzzy
    globe all around me.
It's all too hot except for the cooling bitter-sniff rubbing
    alcohol he spills onto my
        confused form, twisting from the tickle, soaking up
        his icy solution with a moan I
                can't help but create, emit, swallow.

SPRING IN OHIO

Behind the clock was a telephone.

I sat up and then got to my feet.

As if no one had slept there, I switched off the TV

I mustn't have moved, all night long. I dreamt next to, under, my hand,
The Holy Bible, trying to cover myself with it, remembering I was naked

But my hands
kept slipping out of my long fingers.

and bolting for the dresser drawers. Where was the Bible?
I rubbed my eyes and walked to the door.

I could see my breath. Spring in Ohio.

NO ONE BUT ME & GERARD

Me and Bessie and Bessie's sister edging along a narrow cliff, reaching the camp and talking about the cliff. This doesn't matter to me much with my solar panels and in-ground, hidden sound system allowing me to appreciate classical music stoned in the backyard in lounge chair with sunglasses and reflective boards angling the sun at me. My friend Gerard has a wife and three boys and one daughter he calls "Peakee" because of how she used to laugh at the story of me and him on the top of Green Mountain, at the rock top peak, spying those motherfucks through our binoculars, listening, stalking quiet as hell and blasting them with well deserved bullets through their backs. Me and Gerard keep our stories from people like Bessie and Bessie's sister and even little "Peakee" nowadays since "Peakee" is not too little any longer. I just wave goodbye to Bessie and Bessie's sister as they drive away waving back and I wait for a few seconds before I turn around, walk into the front of my house, out the back, and into musical sun-soaked backyard, lying back in lounge chair and draining my head into sunglasses darkened, not a cloud in the blue sky. No one but me and Gerard would understand.

We are still all want and need,

expending spirit and wasting shame.

We apply words (nature doing it through us) that close lids,
cover skin, draw back from hair and spit, scratch semen into
the ground, cover with leaves.

We switch on light bulbs, ignite automobiles, buy and sell
from freezers and pale tubes, strip naked in front of the tele-
vision, write lies, and feed fiction with our fear.
We see subjects where there are no objects.

Naming animals is a sin, after the apple, beyond the
    cracking bones.
Squeezing through, and pushing from, and pressing out.
Imaging life.
Separating one from one and crying to the sky, as if the
    sky were other from us.
But we don't have chaos, and we thank god by saying,
    'Thank god,' to a god that is concealed, but not very well.

Want and need commit crimes that spring from love. We
    hunt to excess.
We make generalizations because we can.
We reduce into categories and we plug into formulas.

Our hearts are seeds pumping out liquid both generative and
deceitful, and the crimes we commit are crimes of
enlightenment imposed.

IN HIS IMAGE

My god
drinks too much
coffee.
Swears he's going
to quit smoking,
someday.

He got duct-taped
to a plywood cross —
Cried so hard
they had to say sorry
and let him down.

ISN'T THAT SWEET?

Rita Reeve: big rig driver. Wednesdays are reserved for coffee and relaxation. Sit back in vinyl recliner. Beat beat beat to the tunes of Brazil. Read the paper, predict the headlines, laugh at morning television — line-ups of freaks, failed families, strippers with complaints, over-weight mothers, psychotic husbands. Eat in silence. Silent lunchtime with sun-striped kitchen table. Open a window and suck in the spring breeze. Two hours in the bathtub, aching legs and fingers. Phone calls to long distance friends — Zachary, Phil, Martha, Steve, Michelle. Everyone's having babies, but not Rita Reeve...

Thursday through Sunday, out on the road. Route 80 West. Through Des Moines, through Lincoln. 76 South to Denver and then 70 West through the mountains. The brakes burn and smoke. Rita eyes the emergency truck ramps. She's never used one yet. Knew a guy who lost control and veered off to save himself, but the rocks and pebbles couldn't hold him. He was going too fast, blew through and up and over. Cut his head off, goddamn. Didn't know him all that well, anyway. Rita knows she'll never have to use one. No fuckin way.

Idaho Springs: used to mine gold, but now it's just a sleepy mountain town. Main strip with laundromat, diner, motel, grocery store, gas station. Rita parks in the Green Grocer lot and heads west on foot. She knows this little place off the beaten path. Lillie's Cafe. A little restaurant with dark wood paneling, lunch counter, good coffee, a heap of bread pudding for 80 cents. Right across from that Szechwan place with the glitter lights. Here we are. Ah, step right in... what the? White walls, calico frilly lace decorations everywhere? Damn, it's bright in here. You got bread pudding? No? Not even on the menu? Jesus.

Soup and a tuna melt. Depressing as hell. Everything's disappearing. Trip across the country ain't what it used to be.

Rita Reeve walks back to the Green Grocer, strolls in, buys a plum and a pack of smokes. First pack in three months. It's too goddamn sad not to smoke. Screams out of Idaho Springs. Got to make time, no more stops. Rita smokes the whole pack in three hours. Her throat hurts and she cries out over her CB radio, "What happened to Lillie's?"

Sunday morning: Rita Reeve wakes up in San Diego. She pays her motel bill and heads out of there. No time for Tijuana. That place is just trouble anyway. Last time she went there she got singled out by a drunk old Mexican lady singing and playing with her hair out in front of the Casa Musica. The mustached owner came over, his sleeves rolled up past his elbows, and ordered the lady to get lost. The crazy lady spit out a couple of swears, as far as Rita could tell. A whole slew of "Boocha, Roocha, Soocha," whatever. Her fists were clenched. The owner turned bright red and flew at the lady, lifting her up off her feet and throwing her about five feet into the gutter. Rita just sat there, drinking her rum. That lady stood up and started throwing chairs into the street. No one paid much attention. When the cops came they just told the lady to calm down, and they went on their way. No ticket, no fine, no nothing. No no no, thought Rita, no Tijuana this time.

Pill-popping Rita took it all the way back to Gary, Indiana, in one long haul. She sang madly along with the radio, slapped the seat, chattered on the CB. She loved the Spanish stations. That Latino sound used to make her laugh every time she heard it, but now it was the only thing on the radio that didn't make her sick. Pop music in the States was bullshit. All of it. Rock, country, dance, top forty. Rita decided that today's American songwriters didn't take

enough drugs. A little marijuana here and there isn't near-
ly enough to stimulate the imagination these days. It
takes heroin, crack, shit-loads of alcohol, and a little
mescaline just to come up with a decent rhythm line. The
Latinos, they were all fucked up. You could tell by the
amazing things flowing out of their instruments.

Back in Indiana, Rita slept for two days, her head spin-
ning out over the highway, reliving the trip home, over
and over. She woke up exhausted and pissed off. Her
alarm clock had been set to go off yesterday. Shit, she
might as well not have pushed so hard on the way home.
Oh well, a pot of coffee set her straight again. It was
Wednesday and the weather was sunny, warm, and
breezy. Perfect. Rita set out on a picnic. She picked up her
pal, Morris, and headed down to Lafayette. She and
Morris had been going on picnics in Lafayette for years
now. They knew this park with green rolling expanses,
paths through dark woods, and a little pond that wasn't
too deep — neither of them knew how to swim. Rita and
Morris had a couple of laughs, ate some food on a red
and white checkered blanket, took a dip in the lake. Then
they walked into the woods and listened for the silence.
They had the whole park to themselves, no one for miles
around. "That's it," shouted Rita and they both stripped
off their clothes, hooting and screeching. They shot off
the path and into the woods, wearing only their boots.
Rita chased Morris up a tree. "Come on down, Morris,"
she whispered, clawing the tree like a cat. Morris clung to
his branch, spying an escape route and lurching over to
another tree. Rita laughed and ran, her arms and stomach
revealing tiny scratches from the pricker bushes all
around. Morris swooped down and chased. The two of
them reached a brook and collapsed. Rita's head soaked
in the icy water while Morris slithered on top of her. Soon

they were a shimmering pile of boots and scratches and wet hair, moaning in tune to the music of the woods.

Down in Birmingham, Rita choked on a chicken bone at the Daniel Boone Truck Stop. She had to be carried away by a couple of locals and dropped off at the hospital. She sat in a bright white room, half-naked, waiting for the doctor to come back. Her throat was clear. No problem. But the doctor had looked at her eyes, listened to her breathing, said, "You don't look good," and left the room. Then there was the nurse with the throat culture and the needle for a blood sample. Rita trusts doctors and nurses, even though they're probably all crooks. Whatever. Click. Door swings open. Pen and clipboard appear, trailed by the clean-shaven doctor. "I'm goin to ask you to stay overnight while we monitor you, Miss Reeve. Yer blood sugar is low, yer lungs are congested, yer heartbeat is irregular, and... well, you got to take better care of yourself with a baby on the way." Baby on the way?

Rita Reeve gets on the phone to Zachary, Phil, Martha, Steve, Michelle: "I'm never coming home. Sell my stuff and send me the money. I just got rid of my cab, bought a nice little trailer outside of Mobile. The weather's great. Water's nice, too. My child's going to grow up on the Gulf of Mexico. My child's going to watch bad TV and eat tuna sandwiches. My child's going to read and write and maybe someday even drive the big rigs. Isn't that sweet?"

NAIL IN M' TOE: A JIG

naked as a dog
as I dance here arms in an arc
an' a footstep
pivot on a bald head
cough an' a choke on a gin an' a hot dog
talk to m' Mom on the phone
she's busy an'
Great Uncle Gizzi is dead with a blood clot
air in m' tires and
smoke in m' lungs
four hours on a bike
in the woods path lost
in a neighborhooda' dead ends
nail in m' toe
right through t' the floor
so pretty soon I find out
just where I am
an' I ride back smack
cause the lungsmoke
don't feel numb in m' head
to a warm light
sink dish read a little
bend down cats on the bath mat
getting lost here with a you and a me
but the TV puts a
nail in m' toe
right through t' the floor
an' I step an' I step an' I step an' I step back
hair in m' mouth
an' I can't breathe easy or speak like I want to
hand on m' job
an' I find great ways to escape but the stick and the stain

on the bed sheet
nail in m' toe
right through t' the floor
an' I can't walk anywhere fine in m' brain
an' I know I'm not alone
but I'm goddamn sicka' this
nail in m' toe
an' I don't know

PUTTING HATS ON BABIES

Dressing up babies
Turning babies upside-down
Talking to babies
Putting babies in commercials
Putting hats on babies
Bringing babies shopping
Making fun of babies
Letting babies know who's boss
Telling jokes to babies
Telling jokes over the phone to babies
Relaxing with babies
Lining babies up for the count
Confiding in babies
Bringing babies to lunch
Bringing babies for ice cream after lunch
Lecturing babies on time and space
Breast-feeding babies
Putting babies in cribs
Imagining what babies will do
Regretting what babies have done
Making babies
Bouncing babies
Dropping babies
Claiming that babies are drunk
Bringing babies to the ball game
Selling babies
Trading babies
Speaking baby-talk to babies
Babying babies
Babying others who, in turn, baby babies
Babying babies who have babied surrounding babies
Baby baby babying baby babies

Buying boots for babies
Assuming that babies believe
Giving babies an even break
Pushing babies in holes
Loving babies
Cleaning babies
Presenting babies
Winning prizes with babies
Debating babies
Concluding babies
Putting babies to bed
Dreaming about babies
Dreaming about babies dreaming about me
And I wonder what kind of hat I'm wearing.

SURPRISE PARTY
(for Joycelyn Elders)

To this day I maintain that masturbation is one of the purist, most exciting art forms known to men and women. It is the most honest expression of simple, generic lust and desire. It is a release, an exercise, a workout, a soul-search, a tune-up, an oil check, a one-man-band complete with bass drum, cymbals, accordion and harmonica. But most of all, masturbation is the most touching affirmation of one's love for oneself.

So naturally, when someone walks into a room and greets me, I politely stop whatever it is I am doing, return his or her greeting with a cheery hello, and begin to masturbate in the most terrific and voracious way. Usually I accompany this act with a powerful and engaging monologue, enumerating my own theories as to the importance and sheer beauty of regular, energetic, public masturbation. My guests will either share their own thoughts on the subject, or sit silently nodding, taking in the whole scene with obvious delight.

On one occasion, I arrived home after a long day at work with visions of bare-breasted co-workers dancing around in my head, each one stripped of her white-collar gar-ments, high heels flying everywhere, skirts unzipped, bra straps snapping all around me. I ran to the fridge for a Fresca and then zoomed into the living room where I sat in complete darkness. I began to enjoy a particularly frenzied session of self-affirmation, my pants at my ankles, when suddenly the lights came on and I was treated to 20 or 30 enthusiastic calls of "SURPRISE!" and "HAPPY BIRTHDAY!"

My god, I thought. I had forgotten all about it. Today was my birthday! Seeing all those cheerful faces made me more excited than ever, and before I knew it I was howling and thumping the floor with my feet. The energy was contagious. Pretty soon a few of the party guests dropped their drinks and joined in on the masturbatory fun. And before long, everyone was doing it, each spiraling off into his or her own erotic fantasies. When it was over, we all had cake and watched movies on the VCR.

I'll never forget that party, and neither will my friends. They still joke about the expression on my face when they first turned on the lights, and about the huge sum of money I had to pay to have the carpet and all the upholstery cleaned. But that didn't matter to me. All I know is that I shared a precious moment with 20 or 30 of the most important people in my life. I thank all of them, and I thank god for giving me two strong hands and a clear path into my own desires, my own frantic, masturbatory fantasy world.

HAIKU MANIA

Regis Philbin jumps
Lands on rotating saw blade
Screams and bleeds a lot

Earthworm crawls from Phil
Donahue's mouth and eats its
Way into his chest

Phil Rizutto you
Crazy fucker. Ride me down
To Memphis. Hee Haw!

Finding out late
That the mind can always snap
If it wants to

Climbing a mountain
Smoking pot at the top
Climbing down happy

Harry hates night
With the shackles on his wrists
And the bug dreams

Clandestine meeting
Jesus Christ and Uncle Sam
Exchange tongues and screw

Clamming on sandbars
My grandfather checks his watch
It's time to go now

LOOKING FOR THE MESSIAH

Sip —
Sip seminal boom!

Hawaiian eyes
Are shining for the
Coming of your lord

Crazy fantasma kite,
Glaring down with bird eyes
Can't even find my faith.

Jimminy Hip Hop
Eats a sock, but
That don't make him no
Bon appétit bing bang
Of a do this do that
Big shot.

WRECKING VISION

A rough trudge toward explosions of sound, signals that slash, practically morphemes, looming close, nearly phonemes, zipping and selectively stirring up meaning, unselecting special blank faces hunched under coat lapels, thickly gloved hands jammed pocketwise, ignoring the flourish, videodeaf to that which, to me, seems a sonic wrecking ball.

Close enough now to see a metal neck scraping, pivoting and bracing its core, scraping its iron straight teeth, crashing its brainless down in sweeps of brick and wirepipe, chunk dust in plumes of gravity shake, fenced in by tight looped aluminum and beerbreak flesh-pods with helmets, tattoos, and arm hair.

Two transfixed faces traced in silhouette behind sunlit glass, and I, with a crack-lipped smile, not now alone, or ever, among the soft drone stepping, vision focused into chain-link tunneling, remembering the monster, clawing down brain gaps and fingering slowly the eggshell tissue flakes, hard hat area, teeth clenched and chattering with cold.

Sun lamp down, faces withdrawn, machines stalled and sleeping, head and fence fused, blanketing now the trash and hum.

THE SEVENTEEN TIMES YOU TOLD ME TO SHUT UP

And the boys and the wires came down for a couple of days to see everything we wanted out of life and to try and figure out exactly what was happening.

And the books and the tires and the things you need to get through each day are looking bigger and bigger all the time and it seems like you'll never get through to the end of anything.

And the righteous citizens of the Seven Cities of Cibola had a master cover-up plan and Coronado was too much of an idiot to find anything anyhow.

And the formula about things like love and dirt and fire and lamps and Hollywood and why everyone hates each other all the time is a little too complicated for me to remember right now.

And every day when I wake up it seems like it's raining or sunny or snowing or windy or overcast or hot or cold and I can tell that there's no way the planet's really round.

And the picket fence I put up around my life today is already coming down because I didn't use the right post-hole digger and it ended up too close to my neighbor's life and he sued me.

And the seventeen times you told me to shut up are finally getting through to me now but it doesn't matter much because I made a promise to myself that I would love everything I do from now on.

SECRET

MY MOTHER

On Thanksgiving my mother comes out to visit. We have a good time cooking piles and piles of food, too much for three people. But my mother says it's a holiday.

DEAN SAYS OKAY, OKAY

Dean sits in his wheelchair all the time, sometimes rolling, sometimes stopped. He looks like he wasn't always in a wheelchair. Dean has a thick mustache and an impressive nose, and he is always laughing or nodding and smiling and saying, "Okay, okay." Dean doesn't come bowling with Lizzy and me. We never invite him, because of the wheelchair. It makes us feel guilty sometimes, to bowl without Dean.

I was the one who introduced Dean to Lizzy. Lizzy is short. The two of them really hit it off; they have a mutual interest in pornography. "Let's plan on going to the Sex-Toy Shop next weekend," she said. "I'm free on Saturday afternoon."

I giggled.

They agreed happily, seriously.

FLIGHT TIMES, DATES

I received a letter from my mother today. She can't wait to get here, knows her new boyfriend will love the coffee shops. He'll love it all. The food is what I look forward to, piles and piles of too much food for, this time, four people.

LIZZY & DEAN

Lizzy says, "Don't give me no battery operated shit. If it don't plug into the wall, I ain't touching it."

Dean adjusts his body in the chair, "Okay, okay. But how do you know that the stuff in other places isn't clean? It's all in plastic..."

"Oh, that doesn't matter!" Lizzy holds her tea cup in both hands, sipping quickly, "You've got to know where to go. You don't want to be shoving some disease infested plastic dowel up your snatch!"

"Okay," says Dean, considering. "Okay."

BOWLING

Lizzy bowls a strike, her first one in seven frames. She raises her arms and hands and blurts out a victory dance. We split a pitcher of beer (best thing to do at the bowling alley). Our waitress is wearing bright purple gauzy pajamas and a black vest. I follow her with my eyes and Lizzy says, "Oooooh baby!" Dean would have laughed.

GROCERIES

The produce section drives us wild. All we need here are potatoes, onions, turnips, apples, and celery; but Lizzy can't keep her hands off the melons. I ride the cart over to the lobster tank. "Poor lobsters."

"What are you talking about?" screeches Lizzy, suddenly by my side. "They're the enemy. It's best to sink one in cold water and then bring it to a slow boil."

We've got the turkey, eggs, two loaves of cheap bread, cream of mushroom soup for the string bean casserole, olives, and Bell's seasoning.

"My mother loves sausage in the stuffing," I say.

Lizzy pulls down on the skin beneath her eyes until she looks like Lon Chaney in *Phantom of the Opera*.

COCKTAIL HOUR

Lizzy shuts the door hard and I head for the bathroom. In the bathroom I pose in front of the mirror, making faces, sticking out my jaw, making noises, "Ugh Ugh Mmm Bbrrr Ugh Ugh." Lizzy shouts from the kitchen, "What the fuck's going on in there!" She laughs. It shakes the walls.

I finish my business in the bathroom. "You been jerking off in there?" She gives herself an imaginary handjob and then runs to the bathroom. I find some rum in the refrigerator and mix myself a drink. "Mix me one!" shouts Lizzy from behind the bathroom door. I mix her a cocktail. I make it strong, stirring it with my finger, and I bring it into the bathroom where Lizzy sits, pants down, on the toilet.

"Here," I say, "drink up." She takes it.

"Now get out," she orders, and I get out.

NEBULAE

"Gallileo was a hot shit," whispers Dean in my ear.

"This is boring," whispers Lizzy in my other ear.

My eyes are fixed on the dome ceiling. It's a small planetarium, but it's the only one around here.

"It's too hot, I'm leaving," says Lizzy, and she gets up.

Dean and I stay till the end. "That was interesting," says Dean as the lights come up and the music fades. "I liked it," he says, and he moves out of the seat and into his wheelchair. I am silent, wondering where Lizzy ran off to.

We take the elevator down and out of the building. It's a nice sunny day. Dean sighs and stretches in his chair. "Well, where do you think Lizzy ended up?"

We head for The Red Fish, a little corner bar about two blocks from the museum and planetarium. I walk and Dean rolls. We arrive at the bar and walk and roll right in. It's dark and smoky and smells fruity.

We find a table and order two double whiskeys and two beers. Lizzy is nowhere to be found. The waitress brings the drinks and Dean thanks her.

"Here's to Lizzy," says Dean, holding up his whiskey.

"Here's to my Mom," I say, remembering that she's scheduled to arrive in two days.

"I'd rather sleep with Lizzy," says Dean, gulping the alcohol and chasing it with beer.

"Me too," I say.

FUDDLED

Head stretch over the toilet blink incinerator. My mother, let me tell you about my mother. And teachers were always so mean. Do you think the future will really look like that? Big translucent atmosphere-regulated bubbles? Shiny people on conveyor belts? The usual white door is so big and so difficult to unlock. "My income is directly proportionate to my handicap." Ha ha ha! "Four more, please." Dean's fingers wash over my galaxy, hot butterscotch melting ice milk. "If you rub toothpaste on your face it stings your eyes something awful." "Really?" Really. Stale breath under mustache, nose like a chisel. Unzip me right here in The Red Fish. The floor quacks red marble, blue fruity crystalline. And my mouth, having sucked all these cigarettes. My mouth, having sucked all this noise and sweaty energy ribbons. "Put it on the credit card."

HELPLESS

"Look!"

Lizzy is pointing at the refrigerator. My eyes are stuck shut. I just woke up and my head feels like it's going to crack. No saliva, either.

"Look!"

Okay, I try to look. Walking up close to the refrigerator, I find that Lizzy's stuck a picture there with a magnet. It's a big, erect penis. Looks like it was photocopied from some magazine. "That's really nice," I say, trying to be sincere.

"Damn right," she says. "That's sweet. Hey, where did you two end up last night?"

I look at her. She's got that look she sometimes gets in the mornings. That manner, it spreads over her whole body. Her hair falls straight on either side of her face, parted in the middle. Her lips are always full and pinkish red without the help of makeup. Lizzy never wears makeup and neither do I. We're proud of that.

"Dean says he'd like to sleep with you," I say.

"Oh," she says, "can you blame him?" And it happens. It always happens fast. Usually when I'm drunk or hung over. The only signal I get is that look in her eyes which leads me to the body, the hair, and the lips. She has a way of jumping up and attaching herself to me, and then it's my job to run for the bed or the couch or to simply slump down to the floor.

THANKSGIVING

"Oh, invite your friend," says my mother. "I'd hate to think of someone alone on Thanksgiving."

My mother's boyfriend sits in the living room reading the morning paper. Lizzy's at the store buying evaporated milk, which we forgot to get.

Now I'm dialing Dean's number. "Dean? Hi. What are you doing today? Why don't you come eat with us? My mom's here with her boyfriend. Lizzy's there? Great, tell her to bring you." I hang up.

"Oh good," says my mother. "Doesn't that make you feel good?"

Actually, it makes me think about pornography. Lizzy and Dean rifling through magazines, videotapes. Greasy fingers ready for any hole. Cheesy lounge music. Stiff dialogue. Tongues and nipples. Extreme close-ups on angry erections. Penetration. Discharge.

THE BEAST

"We did a job on that beast," says my mother, sighing.

"We flattened it," says Lizzy, and she belches.

"Okay, okay," says Dean, picking celery out of his teeth.

"Uuuunnnnngggooooohhhh," moans my mother's boyfriend, holding his abdomen with both hands.

I manage to get to my feet, unable to focus on anything. I stumble through the kitchen and into the bedroom, collapsing onto the bed and curling up on my side. It's time for a nap. I can barely hear conversation.

"I love bookstores. I go all the time. Sometimes I bring Dean with me."

"Really? And what do you do, Dean?"

"Oh mostly I just roll around."

Ha ha ha ha ....

COFFEE SHOPS

My mother loved the coffee shops and so did her boyfriend. When we dropped them off at the airport everybody hugged each other, and my mom said I was the best hugger in the world.

"I'm the best hugger in the world," I say to Lizzy, but she's looking out the front window, watching all the people walk by on the sidewalk. She doesn't hear me. I sip my coffee.

Dean rolls by and looks in and waves.

"Hey, there's Dean!" says Lizzy, and she steps outside to say hi. I notice that Dean is smoking a cigarette.

When I get outside Dean says, "Hear about the coffee shop that went on strike?"

"Yeah, we heard about it," says Lizzy. "It's stupid."

"I didn't hear about it." I don't think Lizzy heard about it, either.

SHADES DOWN

Dean sits up and brushes a fly off his stomach.

"Do you like bowling alleys?" asks Lizzy, rolling over and mussing Dean's hair.

"Sure. I've got the record over at Delmark Lanes; most strikes in a row."

"Last time I bowled, I didn't even get one strike." My back feels stiff so I roll onto my side and curl up.

Dean chuckles and scratches my itchy hip. "It's all in the release."

"You should come bowling with us!" shouts Lizzy, suddenly up on her knees.

"Okay, okay."

It's bright in here. I slip out of bed and reach for the shade. I pull it down.

POLITICAL

If everyone paid just one dollar a day toward the cause of his or her choice.

If everyone did laundry once per month.

If everyone walked out onto the street and vocalized his or her opinions.

If everyone wore jeans and a T-shirt, derby hats and nipple rings.

If everyone ate rotten meat and threw up.

If everyone staked a claim and flushed out the natives.

If everyone sat in the back of the bus.

If everyone sang to the heavens while touching privates.

If everyone had yard sales every day.

If everyone tuned up his or her guitars and waxed his or her skis.

If everyone fell down and then got up and then fell down again.

If everyone whistled Dixie.

If everyone became intimate with close relatives.

If everyone had parties under the stars.

If everyone put his or her garbage in a huge pile on the neighbor's lawn.

If everyone pried the lids off paint cans.

If everyone spit gum at the elderly.

If everyone made lunch and then ate it and then threw it up and then ate it again.

If everyone spent a million dollars on cheap vodka.

If everyone chopped off one finger and gave it to charity.

If everyone remained in stable condition with safety belts secure and seats in their upright positions.

If everyone called lettuce the wonder vegetable.

If everyone agreed that Sparky is the best name for any dog.

If everyone whacked off into an empty swimming pool and
    then bathed in creamy delight.
If everyone got pissed off.
If everyone skipped and hopped and jumped and played.
If everyone watched television.
If everyone gave money and all material possessions to
    children and then made them feel guilty about it.
If everyone got on all fours.
If everyone placed faith and had confidence and hopped
    up and took flight.
If everyone dated someone ugly and stupid.
If everyone grew vegetables and then threw them away.
If everyone just shut up.
If everyone just shut up.
If everyone just shut up.

WORDLYNCH

I don't want to sniff no old poet's soul hole
    sweaty like the day he came out
    and he started to move
    back
    in.

I don't want no doctor of psychological diseases and
magazine covers
Makin it with my telescopic membrane
In the cliff rip
On a metal table in the white
Room
        me
              only in a dress.

It's a back porch thing with me
Kinda puke and potatoes
Salt with tomatoes
I can cook pork roast
    with garlic jabbed in
And clams just come open
    when I dance and parade
And bruised American pie
    that's my specialty
        it's all in the folding
        and the cold iced water

              Sure   I can slide it on over there

or slap it down here,
        with say rays
        flappering that masticating mouth of yours;
        and   I can pull out the tomes,

cry stoned to Olson on the gravelly floor between shelves
wishing for salt breeze and missing the days I played with
myself
 at the Old Lyme cottage, washbin, innocent haircut
 naked streak through living room giggling cousins aunties
 seventies soul music filling the cracks

 in the mind now filling this room and seeping out through
drafty walls,
  My face not fur-filled? These cats not content? This
smile not from love?

 No book this. No Ishmael me. More like Pip, barely able to
keep my air-holes above the surface, the rest of me long gone.

 If my alcoholic Grandma don't please, then I'm content to
sit here with this grilled-cheese and soft drink, screw the rich,
the poor, the felons, the handicapped. I quit smoking, better
than Olson. I quit drinking, better than any one of those
 soul suck
  rot gut
   limp up
    fat old life
     I start reading
      I do 'rithmetic
       look at me now

come a long way since you was arrested caught stealing a pack
of Salems, shook like a sick bird when you stood before the
judge, but he saw you white boy good family (desperate drunk)
scaredand repentant, knew you'd deny it to the end, this was
big stuff sixth degree larceny, and the verdict: "Virgil, twelve
page report, turned into my office by Friday." How many times
felt shamed in the library? Serving time. This is my sentence.

This is how to pay back for all I've done. This is for the touch. That is for the slap.

> don't you motherfuck
> tell me
> you die to write
> before I
> suck the breath
> from cold weak diaphragm
> wordlynch
> king of the mountain

BALANCE ACT

My father and mother always made love in front of me. Ever since I can remember.

At the time, it seemed perfectly natural, and it still does. I see a doctor and he thinks my parents behavior has a great deal to do with everything. But I don't think so at all. I didn't tell him for a long time because I figured he would overreact. At one session, though, he asked me to tell him about my parents, and I was honest about them. He went way off the handle. He started getting nervous and excited, began rifling through stacks of paper on his desk, walked to the bookcase and stared at it hard. He had stopped listening to me and he was looking for something. He kept saying, "We've got something here. This experience of yours. We've really got something." He acted just like I had hoped he wouldn't.

They never touched me. They never involved me. It wasn't anything like that, and I'm offended if the doctor ever insinuates. I walked out on him the first time he mentioned it. He asked me if I ever thought, while the lovemaking was going on, that there might be the possibility of my joining in as I grew older. I said no and I called him an asshole and I left. I went back for the next appointment, and I wanted to explain. But he stopped me and he apologized. He told me why he had said it, and he thought about it and decided he was wrong to have said it, and he wanted me to know that he was sorry he had said it, and he let me say what I wished to say about it, and we talked and we talked and everything was fine.

It was at that same session, after the apologies were over, that we discussed the girl at work and the closest I've ever come to a sexual experience. Believe me, it's not too close. I work at a restaurant, bussing tables, and one of the managers is this girl. She's five or six years older than me, and she sort of acts like the 'mom' of the place, calls us all the 'children' and plays the role of a disapproving mother if any of us misbehave. She always pays attention to me and follows me around and jokes with me when I work. A couple of times, when I was the last one around, she's walked up to me and sort of touched my body with hers and put her face up real close to mine. It always gets to that last split-second moment before I decide I can't help myself from kissing her or touching her, and then she moves back and I'm off the hook and I don't have to touch her.

It doesn't matter to me that she acts like the mom and I'm like the child. That's what the doctor asked, and that's what I told him.

When my parents made love in front of me it was perfectly natural. It wasn't a show or spectacle or anything. They wouldn't make me watch them. But if I happened to be in the same room, they wouldn't tell me to leave. I guess they figured that if I felt uncomfortable, I would leave. And if I was interested, I would stay and watch. Mostly I stayed. I always stayed. But mostly I was just spacing out, looking at the wall, looking at the television screen, putting things in my mouth. I was still very young when they died.

I am convinced that it all stems from the time I decided to lie down on the sidewalk at 72nd Street in front of the Ansonia, and that cop hassled me. My doctor says that there must have been a better reason, a more deeply rooted explanation for my behavior. But I am convinced, and I know for a fact, that I only wanted to look at the sky from the perspective of a New York City street. I wanted to watch the sacs of clouds peek out over the highest ledge of the Ansonia and move across the sky like they were on a slow conveyer belt over New York. And I did. I watched it and people walked by, some walked over. It was kind of funny, and I was doing what I wanted to do and it was a good view of the city, from the city. It made me happier than just about anything I had experienced in my life, and I was relatively happy back then.

It took the cop 20 minutes to get there. I don't know the explanation for his arrival, a random encounter, a tip from an angered pedestrian (one man who hadn't been paying attention tripped right over me, fell on his face, but he wasn't hurt and he was very apologetic, actually). Maybe this cop just knew with his cop intuition that something very bad was going on in front of the Ansonia on 72nd, and when he saw a perfectly content man lying on his back, seeming to enjoy the clouds, acting as if in a moment of real-life perfection, his cop intuition said: This is the guy. Get that smart ass and show him the rules.

He stood right over me and said, "Get up." Then he waited and said, "What's going on? Are you going to get up?" He started fingering his billy club and puffing out his chest, and I could see the sun reflect off the silver pen in his uniform shirt pocket. I asked him if it was against the law to lie on the sidewalk and he said, "Yes!" I asked him if he was capable of reciting or showing me the law in some written form. He didn't say anything. I said that I didn't want to be rude but was it within my rights to remain lying on the sidewalk until he proved to me, without a doubt, that such a law about people and their positions on sidewalks even existed, because I was really doubting that it did. It seemed like a law that he was just making up to fit the situation.

Well, he yelled at me and picked me up by the collar

and held my arm really tight until it hurt and he wouldn't let me explain anything. The more I tried to talk, the more reasonable I became, no matter how calm and polite a voice I addressed him with, the cop just shouted and threatened and shouted and threatened. When I explained my thought that policemen are in a position of authority and that they should never abuse that authority — including things like shouting when it was unnecessary, inflicting pain by holding people's arms, enforcing laws which might possibly not even exist — I thought he was going to shoot me. I really thought he was going to shoot me, and that just shut me up. I stopped talking and I just nodded until he was satisfied. He walked one way. I walked the other.

I've never gotten over that. That stupid feeling of trembling fear, disqualifying reason, canceling rationality. Fear beats intelligent thought. Even the most accomplished intellectual pisses his pants if someone is about to push him off a high cliff. The power to instill fear turns out to be stronger than the ability to be polite.

That's what I try to explain to the doctor. The thing that weighs on me most heavily is the knowledge that negative forces can creep up on you and snap you without a moment's notice, often in the middle of your most cherished moments, always when you expect it least. The doctor says, "What you are talking about is life. These are feelings which everyone must deal with on a daily basis. Everyone. There must be something else at the root of this tendency you have to take the powers of fate so personally."

I do resent the fact that my parents were taken away by something as stupid as a broken axle, pulling them off a busy highway, over a guardrail, into oncoming traffic, into a pickup truck, 60 miles an hour in the opposite direction. The man in the pickup made it through with only a big greenish-purple bruise where he was forced into his seatbelt. It's funny. A seatbelt saves your life, but it stripes you from shoulder to waist with broken blood vessels and damaged tissue. All a guardrail does is to provide you with a ramp into oncoming death. Safety features should be eliminated from this world. Seatbelts should be arrested for assault and battery. Guardrails should be booked on homicide charges. Cops should be more polite, girls should just kiss you if they want to kiss you, not dangle their faces two inches from yours until you're just about crazy, and I should broaden my sexual horizons. I feel like I'm getting old now, and the only thing I have to go on are some hazy memories of my dead parents making love on the living room couch. I try to fantasize about my manager at the restaurant, but it never works. To this day, the only thing that satisfies my desire is the shadowy image of those two beautiful lovers, my naked parents, sinking into each other's bodies, grunting and sighing earnest expressions of affection and deep love... on the brown couch... in my old living room... remembering with the eyes, ears, and thoughts of a young boy... my back to the television... in a dark room... alone... the door is locked... come in my hand... and every time... as soon as it's over... every time... like the expired sign on a parking meter... that cop's face comes swinging into view and he stares at me in my obscene pose.

"Get up," he says. "What's going on here?"

PART**TWO**

Harvis & Malen

TRAGIC MAGIC HAVRIS

That was when their father was sick. She would say,
"Let's go fly our kites, okay? Your Daddy needs his rest."
And then he died at the end of that summer, no more
Daddy, lines of cars driving slowly with their headlights on
in the daytime. Havris and Malen played in the kiddy-
park while friends and relatives paid their respects to the
corpse by throwing rice at long sheets of hammered
aluminum. The aluminum was supposed to symbolize
love and earth, and the rice was supposed to sound like
rain hitting the sidewalk on June 15th when Malen found
himself caught in the middle of a hurricane, crying and
standing in one place, confusing a lesson he learned
about what to do in bad weather with one he learned
about what to do if he ever got lost in the woods. Malen
stood still and called out for people he knew. "Mother!
Mother! Havris! My name is Malen! I'm Malen!" as if he
could out-shout god himself, who was doing a pretty
good job tearing up houses and tossing automobiles.
Finally, Malen's mother, who had been praying over
eggshells in the closet and standing on her rubber mat,
heard the pathetic cries of her six-year-old and shouted to
Havris to go rescue the boy, for Christ's sake. Havris
donned his plastic parka, reluctantly, and ran to save his
silly, confused brother, knocking him onto the ground first
and punching him in the ribs to teach him a lesson which
he would pretty soon confuse with all the other lessons in
his little head. On December 25th Havris turned 40,
and he used the occasion to visit Malen's grave, to
apologize for punching him in the hurricane. "It was
stupid of me," he said. "Sometimes I just got so mad."
And Havris knew that Malen would have forgiven him,
and probably already had, though they never spoke

about it. After all, Havris did save his brother from a hurricane. He dragged Malen onto the front porch where they breathed heavy and watched the storm, huddled together, until it was over. Feel that power. Feel that come around like it does. It comes around and then it does. And when it doesn't come around it makes you think it's not, but then it does and you can feel that power. It's mostly in the fingertips. Havris knows it in his fingertips when he's got the magic. Havris makes the magic happen on everything around him. He touches the couch, the pillows, his books, the television. He stepped up into the sun and looked out from the roof of his mother's house. No more Daddy. Malen followed him to the window, but he was too scared to stick his leg out, reach around, and pull himself up. Havris had the nerve to do anything. He flipped the sky around until it hung below him. He swung from the roof shingles by his toes while he stretched and dipped his fingers into the chalky blue. The sky felt warm, he thought, and just then it stopped. All the blue went still, and it flaked away leaving white patches and cold slither with long cords connecting tree branches and Uncle Manifesto, moving separately toward wet sheets in the plain light of night in slippery sand and one long, whining, distant car horn. His head felt like lead in his hands, and Havris found that he could not look up without everything oozing out into a tragic pile on the grass. It was night, he knew that. And there were faces around. He found himself growling, scuffing the ground with his heels. "Someone call an ambulance." Malen was waiting for him at home, in bed, with a fever of his own. Havris knew, as soon as he opened his eyes the next morning, how ridiculous breakfast was, but he wanted some anyway. He stepped up to Malen's bed and said, "So, you're sick?" Malen's eyes looked puffy and his face flushed pink. "Yeah." Havris smiled from behind a hundred cuts and scratches. Bruises circled his eyes, and dried blood hung from the tip of his nose. "Well, Mom's making breakfast if you want some." He walked out of the room and downstairs, leaving Malen with tiny question marks in his eyes. Three years later, Havris rubbed nervously at the scar under his chin, and he told Malen a story about the man who fell in love with the girl dressed like a hamburger. The man saw her outside of the office where he worked and he just couldn't take his eyes off her. She was rare. She was well done. She was flame-broiled. She didn't use bacon or cheese to attract him. She wasn't that kind of girl. The man asked her on a date. He had to be discreet because he had a wife and two daughters. The girl in the hamburger suit agreed to go out with him, and this excited the man. On their first date, though, the girl showed up in a banana suit. "I needed a change," she implored, but the man walked out on her, dejected. It wasn't the same. Malen laughed and took notes in his spiral bound notebook. Havris stood up and beat his chest, screaming, "I needed a change!" Malen jumped to his feet and joined in. Their chorus filled the house. Their dance was never-ending. Havris bounced from couch to floor to stairs to table, and Malen followed. That whole day twisted around their dance. After two hours the dance became creepy, but they kept on going. "I needed a change!" If only there had been a camera or a tape recorder. The dance became magic after six hours. The two young men sweated and shook, flailing stiff limbs around and laughing out clouds of steam. Their capacities to speak began failing, but they spit out the sounds. "Ah nee cha! Ah nee cha!" The chanting became stronger once they had rid themselves of the jerky words. They touched fingers and elbows.

They kissed the walls and stuffed their feet under cushions and mattresses. The rooms of the house filled with the steam of their energy, and the steam did not choke them, but rather fed them — supplied nourishment and strength. Their lips flared bright red and their eyes sunk into their skulls. "Ah nee cha! Ah nee cha!" Soon the entire house began swelling and pulsating along with the brothers' infectious rhythm. The lights flashed on and off in syncopation with the doorbell, the window screens breathed in the autumn air and blew out magic steam. After nine hours, Havris and Malen found themselves in the basement, exhausted on the cold stone floor. Their chests rose and fell in an eerie synchronization as they slept the sleep of the dead — on their backs, eyes opened and staring into nowhere. Their mother came home crying because she had lost her job. "It's okay," said Malen, massaging her neck with his strong, warm hands. "Ah nee cha," said Havris, and they all laughed.

OUT OF ALL WORLDS

Havris rode his ten-speed down Route 45 with the intention of never coming home.

When he had ridden two miles he paused for a moment and looked back. He balanced his body on the frame of the bike, one foot in contact with the road, his torso twisted. He faced his home and his chest hurt a little at the spot where he imagined his ribs met up with each other. He thought about ice cream.

Havris continued on into the night. He sang to himself out loud. "Pushin too hard. Pushin too hard on me." He felt, happily, that he was out of all worlds. Not even in the world of the bicyclists, with his long pants and black shoes, heavy coat and taped glasses. Havris was no bicyclist, but he loved the escape. Much better than a pickup truck or a freight train. No dharma bum he.

Havris stopped in a dark parking lot at 9 p.m. and pulled a piece of cold chicken from his backpack. Maryann had cooked chicken on Friday night. Now it was Sunday. Good luck, thought Havris as he chewed at the meat. Good luck, Havris.

Three miles down the road Havris picked up a great deal of speed coasting down a steep hill. He withdrew his feet from the pedals and spread out his legs to float on the wind. He looked like an enormous, ill-conceived bird. Not flying but trying. At the bottom of the hill Havris ran smack into a minivan.

The driver of the minivan, Kurt, could not tell what had happened. Was some pesky kid throwing fruit at his vehicle? Kurt continued driving until his girlfriend, Nancy, asked him what he thought he was doing. Was he completely stupid? Did he not even notice the man on the bicycle? The guy he just ran over? "Oh gosh," said Kurt. "Oh gosh," mocked Nancy. Kurt stopped and stepped out of the minivan. He sifted through the darkness with his eyes. Was that him? That lump on the curb? The lump moaned. "There he is!" shouted Kurt, and he ran for the spot.

Havris looked up from his post-minivan-mauling stupor. Whack! A silver hatchback shot by, sending a large, clumsy man reeling and spinning and... Havris tried to roll but the man collapsed in a heap on top of his aching head. Havris felt warm blood from the man's mouth. Blood in Havris's eye. A woman.

"Kurt? Kurt?"

The silver hatchback never stopped, didn't even slow down. Havris and Nancy were married three months later, in December. Maryann was beside herself with joy. Malen was best man at the wedding. Havris and Nancy kept the whole car accident business a secret. Havris limped for a few weeks, blamed it on the weather.

"We've got to find you a job," said Nancy.

"All right," said Havris, playing with Nancy's straight brown hair.

"We've got to make you into somebody."

"Right now I'm nobody."

"The world is so ugly," said Nancy, nodding off to sleep.

"And so big," added Havris.

They were divorced in three weeks.

TULSA OKLAHOMA

Seven p.m. in the icy parking lot of The Ground Street Grill, Havris and Malen drink from a pint bottle of Cutty Sark stolen from the cabinet of Uncle Manifesto. One and a two. T-Rex blasting on the radio. Bright blue Ford Maverick. The two men, drunk boys, light cigarettes and pitch the bottle into a crusted snowbank as they slip out of the car and stand for a moment looking up into the sharp winter sky.

"That's the Pleiades," says Malen pointing and blowing smoke.

"You should watch more television," says Havris. "Come on."

Inside the Ground Street it's dark and warm with smoke and whiskey, beer and chips. Stem, the Irish owner of the place, looks up from the taps, a wide selection of imported beers, and whispers loudly, "A couple a' fags just come in here."

"Two Wild Turkeys and two Millers, please." Havris extracts his wallet for show.

"No Miller! God, you fellows are raw. Put your money away. How about three Wild Turkeys and three Pilsners, on tap? Huh? Miller. Put that away!" Stem slaps Malen's hand and pours the drinks. The three men, drunk boys, guzzle the bourbon and froth their faces with beer.

"You guys want to hear something?" Havris and Malen spun around, spilling their drinks, to face a chubby man wearing a cowboy hat and a bad odor. "I got something for you guys."

The man led them away from the bar, across the dance floor and up to the small stage where an imitation Fender Stratocaster waited patiently in its stand. "My name's Tulsa. Tulsa Oklahoma."

"Glad to meet you. I'm Havris and this is Malen. We're brothers."

"I could tell the two of you were brothers. Believe me, you're in for a treat." Tulsa reached for the guitar. He strapped it over his sweat-soaked shoulders. Havris sipped at the beer he had brought over with him. Malen lit a cigarette.

Suddenly, a spotlight shone on Tulsa. The brothers stepped back, surprised. "What's this?" Quite a crowd had gathered around them. There were chicks in tube tops, dudes in leather vests. Several enthusiastic pimply teenagers held their lighters up in a show of deep respect. Tulsa wrestled a pick from the pocket of his sweat-stained jeans. He strummed a chord and began to sing:

> Hey little darlin with the mule and the cow
> I'm gonna make yer pretty self mine somehow
> An' hell froze over in m' soul that day
> When y' stroked that cow in a personal way
> Pretty soon you n' me
> That's the way it's gotta be
> Here I am on bended knee
> Oh m' little Sarah Lee

"Let's go Malen," whispered Havris. "This is getting scary."

Havris and Malen worked their way through the crowd and back to the bar. Stem stood behind the beer taps beaming. "Isn't he great? Just walked in this morning and guaranteed he'd draw a crowd if I let him play. We haven't been this busy for months."

"Where did all these people come from?" asked Malen.

"Don't know. It was like they all just materialized. They're big drinkers! God this is good."

"Hey Stem, you got anything to go?" asked Havris, leaning over the bar.

"What'll it be?"

"How about a bottle of Jim Beam and a six-pack of Miller?"

"You got it," and Stem handed over the booze.

Havris leads Malen out the door and into the icy parking lot. Malen looks into the sky and says, "What was that all about? Did Stem even charge you for that stuff?"

"No," says Havris, pulling Malen toward the car. "It was like he was hypnotized. There's some kind of magic. Didn't you feel it? The best thing for us would be to get in that car and drink all this alcohol."

"Excellent," says Malen. "We'll drive out to the Strapp River. I know where we can get a gun."

Havris laughs and points an index finger to his head. "Pow!" Malen unlocks the car door and plants himself behind the steering wheel. He reaches over to unlock the passenger door. Havris slides into the car and twists open a Miller. The Maverick starts with some effort. "Man, it's cold." They pull out onto Route Six headed west.

"You guys oughtn't to joke about things like that." Havris and Malen jolted to attention. Malen peered into the rear view mirror. There he was.

"What are you doing here, Tulsa?" asked Havris. "Isn't your gig still going on at the Ground Street?"

"Well yeah it's going on. You think I'd leave my fans in the lurch?"

"So you can be in more than one place at the same time?"

"I don't know about all that," said Tulsa, withdrawing

a harmonica from the pocket of his green Nylon jacket.
"But I do know a song I'm sure you'll both find inspiring."

And he sang:

> If y' joke about things like killin yerself
> Well it can't be good fer yer spiritual health
> Drinkin that booze an' drivin around
> A car wreck makes a terrible sound
> (harmonica solo which sounds like a car wreck)
> > Oooh doggy
> > Whoah Nellie
> > Y' might as well put a bullet in yer belly

Havris, who had drained his beer during the song, went for the Jim Beam. He ripped at the seal and unscrewed the cap. "Listen, Tulsa. I'm sure you mean well, but my brother and I are just trying to have a good time. We can do without the public service announcements."

MALEN

Rummaging through piles of dusty magazines,

this is not my house. The people who ever made this my house are gone, and it's not that I don't

think so

about it.

Well, isn't this fun? Tricking foresight out of its never be tricked out of never being tricked out of foresight? And all because of this

                                 body
(vague piece of rag, suffering to be stretched over this old shoe, disintegrated by chemical polish, surrendering its own fibers, working to become part of the polish, the shoe, and finally fading, on display down there, five hundred and sixty-four steps from this building to that, and kicking a can or pebble quickens the) loosening and forgetting patterns, ways;

regardless of how many attics, whose faces I see, what time of day   it is.

Does it count if I work at my sorrow three hours into your chest? If I cry and let it ripple out of me, does it count? Does this lump under the skin of me tell you something that it doesn't whisper to me before sleep?

Is it heroic to cry
for you? Does it become repetitive? Is it a drag? I think of
my brother, my older brother, Havris, puking up tears in
the only way he knew, in the car, just before dropping
him off, myself in a hurry for you and a film, dusk, dash-
board blue and so was he as he let me have it "I'm
tired" in a wash and blur of stepping up, out, walking
away and myself using the reverse, the brake, the drive

before the door slammed and after "I know"
before the door slammed and after "I know"

ABOUT CRYING

Malen cries more than most men. Malen cries because he thinks he has something to cry about. If not his own bug dreams, then those experienced vicariously through Havris. If not his own car accident, then that of Havris. If not his own drug addiction...

The handlebars are as far as Malen's head has gone, never over, never smashing on concrete, although we cannot deny that he risks it. Malen is not scared of experience. Malen is known to drive stoned, to insult big guys, to have unprotected sex. Malen is a hero to some, a zero to others. He has a crooked smile. His eyebrows are too big. He smokes cigarettes, all the while slapping himself for doing so. Across the face in the cold. Smack!

Havris has normal eyebrows. He is older than Malen and better looking. If Havris cries it's for a reason. If he drinks too much he badgers people about his family: "My mother is a good woman. Maryann did her best by us. That Hal fucked her over. Was it her fault?" If Eli asks him to change the subject, Havris winks and smiles and sucks it all up into his throat, leaves it there to be puked up in the morning.

Malen realizes that there is not enough time in the day to do the things he wants to do. So he gives up and decides to watch television. All his free moments are filled with space.

Havris remembers smoking cigarettes with his younger brother, drunk, sneaking into a mostly empty drive-in and sitting next to a speaker pole, lecturing his younger brother on feelings and hurt, claiming that he is not responsible for any of Malen's future delinquency, leaning on Malen, inviting Malen to lean on him. And all the while, that little Spielberg alien rifled through a refrigerator on the big screen. Havris laments about years spent drunk, drugged, hiding from the sun. But he does not cry.

Malen cries the first time he sees *Conquest of the Planet of the Apes*. Malen cries in the middle of an open field in Mansfield, Connecticut. Malen cries in the car on his way home from a late night party. Malen cries about his mother and her screwed up decisions. Malen cries about the dog, crushed by a truck. Malen cries for the Lebanese. Malen cries when his VCR breaks down.

Havris reaches back and touches himself, naked.

Maryann tells little Malen that he's a sissy. Malen cries even harder.

Havris, drunk, stares at his hacked face in the bathroom mirror. He holds the razor up and then puts it down. Holds it up, puts it down. Havris cannot walk by an open silverware drawer without feeling sorry for the spoons, the neglected spoons. He sits in Maryann's car and runs the engine, garage doors closed. Malen cries about this.

HAVRIS & ELI

The cops are just outside my apartment but all I can think about is Eli, the guy I work with at the ice cream shop. He's so thin and he's gorgeous and he always talks about old television shows and smiles at me. Once I caught him prodding at his stomach. I asked him what he was doing and he looked embarrassed. He said he was trying to push in his stomach because he didn't like the way it looked.

On our first date he told me he loved me and that he knew it was stupid to feel that way on a first date and that I couldn't possibly feel the same way and that he probably ruined any chance I had for loving him by making such a strong statement so early in our relationship. I said, "No, I love you, too." And I bought him some french fries and a seltzer water at the Dairy Queen. He kept smiling at me but every once in a while he'd go into these crying fits that were so violent he could barely speak a word. And when he managed to say anything it would be something like "everything's ruined" or "I can't keep going" or just "help me."

But it was nice, in a way, to have someone so emotionally distraught around. I've never been able to handle anything in my life, but next to Eli I seemed secure.

And his cooking was amazing. He'd prepare the most extensive dinners, the table filled with salads and bread and pasta and fruit and potatoes and sauces. But he would never touch the food he cooked. Once he just sat at the table eating Sweet Tarts. I'd try to eat as much of the food as I could, because I knew he would throw out whatever was left over. He'd ask if I was finished and when I'd say yes he would start clearing the table, dumping platters of roast pork, half-filled bowls of mashed potatoes, whatever was left of the butter, all into the trash. When I asked him why he never kept the left-over food he just looked at me like I was trying to embarrass him.

The day after our first date, I saw him at work. He was leaving and I was just starting my shift. He didn't say anything. He just counted his money, did his sales report and left. He only looked at me once and I couldn't figure out what he was thinking. When he left I said, "See you later," but he just sighed and walked out with his big bag over his shoulder. He looked incredible and I couldn't help smiling.

He called me later that night. We talked from 7:35 until 9:15. At first I asked him if he'd call me back since I was busy with everybody buying sundaes and floats, but he said he didn't mind if I was busy and he wouldn't bother me just as long as I kept the phone to my ear. I said, "Okay," and for the next half hour I sold ice cream and took care of all my customers with the phone pressed between my head and shoulder. I didn't say anything except for an occasional "thank you" to a customer and whenever I'd say that I could hear Eli chuckle. I could also hear a television in the background. It sounded to me like he was watching *The Land Of The Lost*. I could swear I heard the theme song three times, and all along there was the hissing of the Sleestacks. But when I asked him, he denied it. I spent the rest of the phone call accusing him of watching *The Land Of The Lost*, but he never admitted a thing.

Before we hung up he told me he loved me again, and I told him I loved him. For the rest of the night I tried to imagine Eli in front of his television.

SORTING

"It reminds me of ten seconds."

"It reminds me of the three minutes before the fall."

"Before the fall?"

"Yes. A sleepy back and forth. The head propped up against painted wood meeting brick. A trusting, sleeping hand edging its own way along the seam of worn-out jeans."

"It reminds me of ten seconds."

"What, swaying and misplaced legs? One moment with an open eye? Finding a jolt of lost balance?"

"Yes."

"Flight and falling and still half asleep or still all asleep and then stop?"

"I guess it stops suddenly."

"It reminds me of the quiet and the early morning New York peace, before the ten seconds. I hate to think of it as a count down."

"Well, that's what it was, really. A countdown until it all stopped. Ten... nine... eight... seven..."

"Stop it."

MALEN IS DEAD

If Malen is dead, well that's his own damn fault. If Malen can't keep himself from falling out of windows, it's not my problem. I enjoy the smack of your boy lips and your boy tongue against my cold ear. You know I do. It crackles and makes me warm with you. There's no use in hanging around here, let's go.

The cold air and dusty white outside this car. It is President's Day and you don't even act accordingly. I tell you about my card collection — all the presidents up to Nixon. I lost interest after Nixon. Penis-nose! you say. You laugh and your laughter makes me want to drive the both of us off this road. Over guardrail. Into ditch. I tell you it's not all right with me. Big deal, you say. That makes me laugh.

I worry about the clothes I'm wearing. These socks and what they say to the public. My sweater is form fitting. Do you like the shoes? Are they too...?

"The problem with you, Havris, is that you don't watch enough television."

"The only reason I don't watch television, Eli, is because I haven't got one."

"That's no excuse."

I worry about you, Eli, and the way you think. When Malen was growing up I had complete confidence that he could follow me. He could follow me wherever I went, and we would be just fine. I remember him trailing after me, the two of us crawling under the gate to the drive-in. I gave him a cigarette because he asked, not because I wanted to corrupt him. He wanted to do it all — to smoke and drink, to stay up all night and walk around dangerous neighborhoods. Girls loved him, so did boys.

"What is this film?"

"*E.T. The Extra Terrestrial*."

"Oh yeah, Spielberg."

"Spielberg's a chump. He's getting rich off a muppet."

"Turn on your heart light."

"Fuck that."

Your hand feels warm on my wrist. I look at your face and see Malen, pale and crazy-eyed. What are you thinking about? you ask. It makes me want to cry and so I do. Your fingers run through my hair. I know you're trying to comfort me, but it's the same every time. I hate being touched on the head. You know I hate it.

I step away from the grave and you touch me, place your arm around my hip. I fall into you, crying. I look into your eyes, which dart around defensively. This show of affection is not unusual for us, Eli, but all the relatives you've never met, huddled together in the cold, wearing black, staring openly at the spectacle, mournful and disapproving. You guide me to Maryann who stands shivering with tears and the cold.

"If you wanted to make a scene, why didn't you just throw yourself on the coffin?" Bitter icicles trail down her cheeks.

"Let's go," you say, and we stumble for the car.

Havris notes two anemic nipples, tugs on tufts of hair, smears anti-perspirant into bushy armpits. He breathes in steam and blows out dust, feels winter frost outside the drafty bathroom window, wipes away his own reflection from the mirror. "Here I am again. I've been here before." Havris reaches for his toothbrush and begins brushing without toothpaste or water. Begins brushing without logic or intent. His gums respond to the abrasive attack, first tingling and then swelling. His gums ask him to stop, but secretly they dare him to go on. Go on. Go on and make us bleed. We bleed and we are your gums and we let go of these teeth and it's finally time to be free of the smell of living and rotbreathing and we slide from this skull and it's too much. "I've been here before." Havris rinses the toothbrush and places it on the rim of the sink. He opens the medicine cabinet, withdraws a bottle of antiseptic, closes the cabinet, and suddenly he is there. He stares at himself in the mirror. Tries to wipe. His eyes are red and full of tears, but he is not crying. He uncaps the antiseptic and lifts it to his lips, tilts back his head and swallows three times. Tilts again and swallows three times. Tilts again. "Malen's never been here. It's a place I've made for myself." Havris kneels down beside the bathtub and begins to pray. This porcelain temple, soap scum, pubic hair clogging the drain, the acrid scent of deodorant. Havris prays for himself. He prays against the world. Carbon monoxide, razor blades, shotguns, nooses, sleeping pills. Somewhere out there the telephone rings. Havris shifts his weight and sits with his back against the tub. Three more rings, a few seconds of silence, and then: "Havris? It's a place you made for yourself, that's true. You may think I've never seen it, but I have. You showed it to me and I think it's fine. Don't worry about it so much." Click. Havris chuckles. He stretches out his arms, knocking the antiseptic bottle into the tub.

Cousin Leonard wears white socks with black shoes and he smells like burnt plastic. He is known for his incessant chatter. He'll talk your ear off if you give him a chance. He is an old man and he is all alone. The only time we see him is at funerals.

"It's a shame what happened to your brother. He was so young. I remember him as a clever young thing."

Eli squeezes my hand and gets up from the couch to

find a drink. Cousin Leonard looks at him cross-eyed, betraying his discomfort.

"I'm so sorry for you and your mother. The three of you were very close, weren't you?"

I lean forward and select a piece of cheese and a pepperoni slice from the hors d'oeuvres tray on the coffee table. I motion to Cousin Leonard.

"No, no. None for me. I've got to watch my weight." He pats his swelling belly, smiles ironically and then looks into my eyes. He expects me to say something.

"Well, you're fat already. You've been fat since I've known you. Why don't you go ahead? The cheese is very good." I chew excitedly, waiting for his response.

"When you put it that way, how can I refuse?" Cousin Leonard leans forward and reaches a stubby arm toward the coffee table. He is unable to reach the tray from his position on the couch and so he begins to rock backward and forward until, on the third try, he manages to snatch a piece of cheese. "You're right," he says, depositing the cheese into his mouth and settling back into the couch. "It's delicious."

"Cousin Leonard," I begin, inspired by my wave of frankness, "how do you suppose someone manages to fall out of a window? Six stories up. No one else in the room. No high winds or any other adverse weather conditions. How does someone manage to just... fall out?"

"We're all a little confused by it. It was a terrible accident. Things happen in this world. Some things are horrible and disgusting, and other things are very good and beautiful. Malen lived the best life he could, and when his time came..."

Eli returns with two glasses of water. Both Cousin Leonard and I look up at him in a moment of solemn silence. He hands one glass of water to me and I take it, guiding him back to his place on the couch. The interruption breaks my concentration, and my head spins out over the spirals of quiet. The room becomes strangely warm and liquid. I look into Eli's eyes and he looks into mine. I can't help myself from touching his face, from smelling his hair, from kissing his forehead, from suddenly weeping and holding him close. Closer.

"Oh my," says Cousin Leonard, my glass of water spilling into his lap. He begins his slow retreat, rocking backward and forward until he can jettison himself from the couch.

DEAR MALEN,

Since you asked, I'll tell you. The feeling starts from
somewhere not inside me. It starts from somewhere dark,
somewhere cold and exposed. I guess it's just chance
whether it falls on you or not. It brushes up to almost
everyone, causing a tinge of hate or sadness when it
does, but it also throws its full weight on some people,
and that's what I think it's done to me. Everywhere I look
I feel sad and sorry that the objects around me must suf-
fer through this life. If I press a sharp razor into the veins
in my wrist, sure it'll hurt, but the feathers and moons
and spaces between branches and leaves can all escape in
one gush not like an orgasm but like an avalanche that
snaps your head before you suffocate in the snow. You
see, it's like I don't have any legs. When dogs walk by me
and lift their noses to the sun all I can see is the yellow
sputum around their eyes, the plaque caked on their
teeth. To throw myself in front of a train would be the
beginning of a frenzied game that maybe I won't win,
but winning isn't the point. Winning would only bring
sadness for the others who've lost. Remember the hat I
used to love? It fell out of the car and Maryann wouldn't
stop, right? Do you remember how I reacted? Well it was
bad, it felt like my lungs had been sucked out of my chest
and left back there. Back there with my hat. My hat had
gone into some void. I knew that if we didn't stop then
and there that I would never find it again. Malen, I still
cry about the hat. Every day I think of it. Maybe you
don't understand. I have trouble walking because I feel
like I'm punishing the soles of my shoes. If my shoes wear
out, there is more and more pressure to get rid of them,
to throw them away after all they've done for me. If my
hair touches anything, any surface, I know that I'll die. It's

like when you graduate high school and you know that you won't see any of these people you hate any more, and it's sad. I get drunk and start fights so I can get punched in the face. I smash Maryann's car over and over because I want a reason to cry. I want a reason to cry because it's a substitute for letting all the blood out of my body. I want to cry blood. Don't you see? Haven't you ever felt like that?

Love,
        Havris